What I Love Most

journal belongs to...

© 2016 Ranch House Press
All rights reserved. Printed in the United States of America.

www.annettebridges.com

ISBN: 978-0-9981576-4-1

Journal Prompts

What I LOVE Most

1. What was your favorite childhood toy? What did you love about it?
2. Who was your best friend in elementary school? High school? College? Now? What did you love about them?
3. What was your favorite subject in school? Favorite teacher? Why?
4. What books have you read over and over again?
5. Describe the holiday traditions you most look forward to.
6. Make a list of 100 things you love and why. Your list might include activities, restaurants, people, foods, games, hobbies, beverages, desserts, paintings, websites, authors, book movie and song titles or famous lines from books/movies…
7. Name three things you can't live without.
8. What are the three most important things you want in a relationship.
9. Your three favorite things to wear are…
10. Who are the people you most admire and why?
11. The top ten things you appreciate in life are…
12. (Fill in the blank) I love to…
13. Your favorite way to spend the day is…
14. Make a list of thirty things that make you smile.
15. Who do you love unconditionally? What does unconditional love look like to you?
16. Write about your first love — whether a person, place or thing.
17. You feel most energized when…
18. What inspires you? From books to websites to quotes to people to paintings to the stars…
19. What activities excite you?
20. When you were ten years old, what did you dream of doing?
21. What motivates you? Look at the times you did a task, made a commitment or fulfilled a task with boundless energy. Describe the circumstances.
22. What would you do in life if you did not need to work for money?
23. What is happiness for you?
24. Pick an everyday item you love or especially enjoy and use all of your senses to paint a word picture. Describe it using five visual descriptions. What does it look like, how does it feel, how does it sound, how does it smell, how might it taste?
25. State one line from a movie that makes you laugh or smile every time you hear it or a line that you quote frequently. Do you remember it because of the film or because of the people you were with? How would you persuade someone else to see the movie?
26. Describe your perfect view. Create a collage of images; cut and paste magazine pictures that depict your perfect view.
27. Imagine your best party ever. What would the theme be? Decorations? Food? Music? What elements would make it your ideal party?
28. Pretend you just walked into a coffee shop and "that" song was playing. That song that always evokes special beloved memories. What song is it? What event does the song remind you of and what people do you associate with it?

color your world

ABOUT the CREATOR

Annette Bridges is an author, publisher and women's retreat host on a mission to help every woman realize her story is extraordinary, valuable and noteworthy.

She has published the *Color Your World Journal Series* and formed a journal club to provide community, support and tools for women to record their ideas, feelings, experiences, memories and all the important details of their lives.

Before writing books and publishing journals and coloring books, this former public school and homeschool educator spent a decade writing hundreds of helpful, instructive, and light-hearted columns published by Texas newspapers, parenting magazines, websites and bloggers.

Annette lives on a Texas cattle ranch with her husband John, dachshund Lady and lots of cows. She can drive a tractor but only if wearing a fresh coat of lipstick and it's not her pedicure day!

You can learn more about Annette's books and products, blogs and videos as well as her women's retreats and other events at www.annettebridges.com.

Look for her on social media, too!

MESSAGE from the PUBLISHER

The **Color Your World Journal Series** is a pathway to self-discovery. It's where you write notes to yourself. Be your own cheerleader. Give yourself encouragement. Tell yourself what you're grateful for. Celebrate you!

There are countless reasons to keep a journal including collecting favorite recipes, listing goals and celebrating every experience and every one that's near and dear to you. A journal provides a home for the memories and lessons learned that you never want to forget.

Why a niche journal?

If you're anything like me, you have a journal (or even two or three journals) where you write anything and everything about anything and everything. My challenge comes when trying to find something I've written. I flip and flip through the pages of my two, three or four journals trying to find whatever it is. I never remember which journal I wrote down my whatever's!!

The solution? A niche journal! A journal that has a specific focus and theme! A journal where you can record your ideas, inspirations and things you want to remember in the appropriate journal.

Why big unlined paper?

Because big unlined paper is needed to record big ideas, dreams and memories! You need room to grow, stretch and expand. You need space to think beyond the confines of what you've always done, to pursue new dreams, discover your power and reimagine your purpose again and again. You need pages without lines and limitations to reconnect with your creative, perfectly imperfect self.

Plus, big unlined paper gives you space for more than words. You have plenty of room to doodle, draw or post photographs and clippings, too.

Why color is important?

When you journal, use colored pens and markers! Your world doesn't happen in black and white. Your life should be lived and written about in many colors. Even dark and sad memories feel lighter and brighter when told in color.

Journaling in color affects your mood and perception of your world. Colors evoke calm, cheer and comfort. Using color can lift your spirit and inspire your imagination. You may be surprised by all the beautiful benefits from adding more color into your life story.

When journaling, give yourself time to listen to your heart and reflect. Breathe in the moments. Feel. Be quiet. Let yourself be totally and thoroughly present with your thoughts. Let your heart transform you and teach you new insights. Open your mind to consider new ideas and possibilities. You may find that what your heart teaches will be life changing.